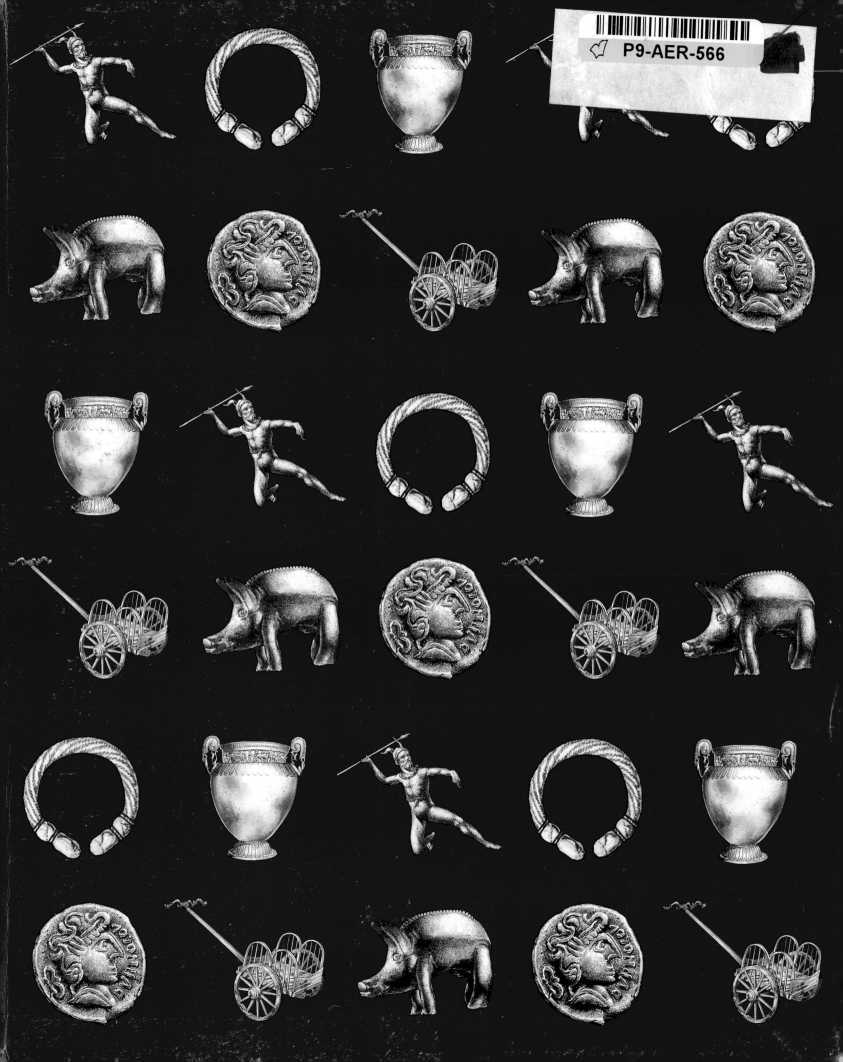

THE
CELTS

HAZEL MARY MARTELL

Acknowledgments

The publishers would like to thank Mrs. M. Fry at Historic Scotland, and Nick Brannon and Anne Hamlin at the Department of the Environment for Northern Ireland, for their assistance in the preparation of this book; Bill Le Fever, who illustrated the see-through pages; and the organizations that have given their permission to reproduce the following pictures:

Archiv für Kunst und Geschichte/Eric Lessing: 4-5, 5 top, 9 center bottom, 12-13.
Ancient Art and Architecture Collection: 24 top, 27 bottom right, 34 top, 45 top right, /Ronald Sheridan 10 top, 11 top, 13 bottom, /Brian Wilson 9 top right.
Bibliothèque Nationale: 34 bottom, 38 top left. **Bridgeman Art Library/British Museum:** 20 top left.
British Museum: 15 top, 18 top left. **C.M. Dixon/Photo Resources:** 23 top right.
Explorer/A. Le Toquin: 27 center right. **Historisches Museum Basel/M. Babey:** 29 bottom right.
Historic Scotland: 32. **Simon James:** 23 bottom left. **Life File/Tony Abbott:** 14 top.
The Menil Collection /Hickey-Robertson: 27 center left.
Moravske Zemske Muzeum: 27 bottom center. **Musée d'art et d'histoire, Geneva:** 31 bottom right.
Museum Carolino Augusteum, Salzburg: 12 top. **National Museum of Ireland:** 21 center.
National Museums of Scotland: 45 bottom right. **National Museum of Wales:** 28 top left.
Photographie Giraudon/Chatilloon-sur-Seine, Mus. Archeologique: 21 bottom right, /Musée des Antiquites Nationales, Saint Germain en Laye 9 center top, /Rueil-Malmaison, Mus. Nat. de Château de Malmaison 43 top right.
RCS Libri & Grandi Opere Spa/Muzeul National de Istorie a Romaneiei: 37 top left.
Réunion des Musées Nationaux/Musée des Antiquites Nationales: 19 top right, 27 top.
Scala/Rheinisches Landesmuseum, Bonn: 7 bottom, /Museo del Terme, Rome 39 right.
Society of Antiquaries of London/Geremy Butler: 5 bottom right.
Ville de Beaune, Conservation des Musées/Musée du Vin de Bourgogne/M. Couval: 23 top left.
Werner Forman Archive/British Museum: 8 bottom right, 9 top left, 13 top right, 35 bottom, 37 top right, /National Museum of Ireland 31 top right, /National Museum of Wales 27 bottom left.
Württembergisches Landesmuseum: 25 top.

Illustrators
Richard Berridge: 28, 29, 30-31, 36, 37.
Peter Bull: 7, 29, 38.
James Field: cover, 42, 44, 45, 46-47.
Ray Grinaway: 8, 9, 10, 11, 20, 21, 43.
Bill Le Fever: heading icons, 16-17, 24-25, 32-33, 40-41.
Tony Randall: 12, 13, 14, 15.
Mark Stacey: 4, 6, 18, 19, 34, 35.
Simon Williams: 22, 23, 26, 38-39.

Published by the Penguin Group
Penguin USA, 375 Hudson Street, New York, New York 10014, U.S.A.
Penguin Books Ltd, 27 Wrights Lane, London W8 5TZ, England
Penguin Books Australia Ltd, Ringwood, Victoria, Australia
Penguin Books Canada Ltd, 10 Alcorn Avenue, Toronto, Ontario, Canada M4V 3B2
Penguin Books (N.Z.) Ltd, 182–190 Wairau Road, Auckland 10, New Zealand

Penguin Books Ltd, Registered Offices: Harmondsworth, Middlesex, England

First published in Great Britain by Hamlyn Children's Books,
an imprint of Reed Children's Books Limited, 1994
First published in the United States of America by Viking,
a division of Penguin Books USA Inc., 1996

1 3 5 7 9 10 8 6 4 2

Copyright © Reed International Books Limited, 1994

Library of Congress Catalog Card Number: 95–61265

ISBN 0–670–86558–3

Printed in Belgium

CONTENTS

THE FIRST CELTS

Long ago, before Rome became a power in the ancient world, the people we call the Celts dominated much of Europe. Their influence ranged from Britain and Ireland in the north to France and Spain in the south to the Balkans and Turkey in the east. They were united not by a common ruler but by a common language and culture. Though it is now many centuries since their power declined, the influence of the Celtic culture and language remains.

Early Celtic traders leave their homes near Hallstatt to go to Greece. They took blankets and hunting equipment in addition to their trading goods since they had to sleep in the open and catch any food they needed.

> **Almost all the Gauls are of tall stature, fair and ruddy, terrible for the fierceness of their eyes, fond of quarreling and of overbearing insolence.**
>
> — *Ammianus Marcellinus* —

EARLY TRADERS

The Celts first appear in history in central Europe in the eighth century B.C. Celtic traders crossed the Alps from Hallstatt, in what is now Austria, to trade with the ancient Greeks on the shores of the Mediterranean. The Greeks called them *Keltoi*. This word was probably based on the name the Celts used to describe themselves, since the Romans also called them *Celtae* or *Galli (*Gauls*)*, but we cannot be certain because the Celts of this time left no written records.

ABOUT THE CELTS

However, scholars from Greece, and later from Rome, left descriptions of the Celts and of how they lived that we can still read today. Both the Greeks and Romans thought the Celts were uncivilized. This was because the Celtic way of life was so different from their own. The Romans often referred to them as barbarians, and believed them to be a war-loving people who indulged in grisly human sacrifices. They were determined to conquer them and make their lands part of the Roman Empire.

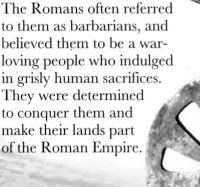

ARCHAEOLOGICAL EVIDENCE

More recently, we have been able to build a different picture of the Celts, based on the work of archaeologists. By excavating Celtic sites and studying the artifacts left behind, archaeologists now know that the Celts were successful farmers and traders, as well as fierce warriors. They were skilled at making cloth, and at mining and working with metals to make tools, weapons, jewelry, and ornaments. Unlike most people who lived during Celtic times, they cared for the sick and poor members of their tribes. They were also great storytellers. They learned their legends by heart and passed them down from one generation to the next by word of mouth.

This bronze container, in the form of a wheeled vehicle and two birds, was made in the seventh century B.C. About seven inches long, it probably held food or drink. It was found near Sarajevo, in the former Yugoslavia.

HISTORY AND PREHISTORY

The times before people started writing a record of events are known as prehistory. In the 19th century archaeologists tried to create an accurate timeline for this period by dividing prehistory into three ages. These were based on the materials people used for their most important tools and so there was a Stone Age, a Bronze Age, and an Iron Age. Because the Celts used iron for most of their tools and weapons, they belong to the Iron Age. The Iron Age itself has since been divided into two periods, based on two collections of Celtic artifacts excavated from sites at Hallstatt, in Austria, and La Tène, in Switzerland.

HALLSTATT AND LA TÈNE

Hallstatt was the older of the two sites and most of the artifacts found there dated from between the seventh and fifth centuries B.C. They were excavated from over 1,000 graves belonging to people who had become wealthy through mining and trading salt. The site of La Tène on the shores of Lake Neuchâtel was probably occupied from the middle of the fifth century B.C. until the local Celts were conquered by the Romans in about 15 B.C. This is the period when Celtic culture was at its peak and is the time we will look at most closely in this book.

Although iron is a much stronger metal than bronze, it is not as easy to work with. Therefore the Celts continued to use bronze to make fine objects such as this stand, which was found in a grave at Hallstatt.

Between 1846 and 1863, archaeologists excavated a cemetery at Hallstatt that contained over 1,000 graves. They recorded their findings in detailed watercolor paintings.

CELTIC EXPANSION

The iron tools used by the Celts were stronger than the earlier wooden and stone tools had been. This enabled the Celts to clear more land for farming than any of the peoples who had lived in central Europe before them. As they brought larger areas under cultivation, there was more food for people to eat, and the population began to increase. This, however, led to overcrowding, and some families were forced to find somewhere else to live.

It must have taken migrating Celts a long time to prepare for their journey. As well as household goods and food, they needed tools for farming and building, and seeds from which they could grow new crops.

THE FIRST MIGRATIONS

The early Celts at first looked for land to farm along the fertile valleys of the Danube and Rhine rivers. From there they spread out north, east, and west, and by the sixth century B.C. they had started to colonize the lands we now call France, Belgium, and Spain. Other Celts had braved the English Channel and settled in the British Isles. Celtic tribes also crossed the Alps and settled in the valley of the Po river in northern Italy.

We can only guess at the difficulties faced by these early travelers. They would have been laden with their possessions, and hampered by their livestock. They had no maps to guide them, no knowledge of the lands they traveled through, and they would almost certainly have met with resistance from their new neighbors!

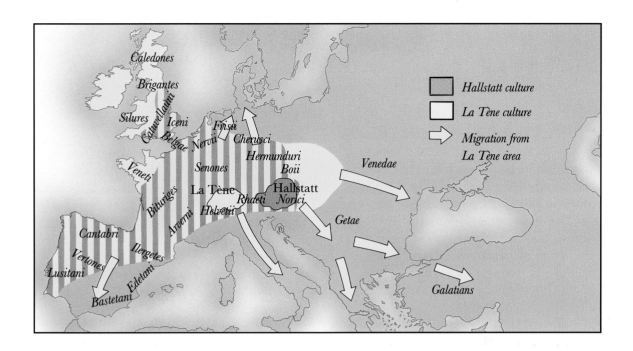

Map legend:
- Hallstatt culture
- La Tène culture
- Migration from La Tène area

EXPANSION IN THE EAST

As you can see from the map, the Celtic population continued to expand. By 358 B.C. some of the Celts were living as far east as the Carpathian mountains. Fifty years later, others had settled in Moravia, in the former Czechoslovakia. In 278 B.C., 20,000 Celtic families went to Asia Minor to assist Nicomedes, the ruler of Bithynia, in his fight against the Syrians. These Celts were known as the Galatians. When the fighting was over, they settled in a region still known as Galatia (part of modern Turkey). In 277 B.C. around 4,000 Celtic mercenaries traveled to Egypt to fight for the pharaoh, Ptolemy II. Some probably made their homes in Egypt, too.

CLASHES WITH ROME

While the Celts were spreading out to the south of the Alps, the Roman Republic was also growing more powerful. The Romans and the Celts could not live in peace with each other, and around 390 B.C. their armies fought at a place called Allia where the Romans were utterly defeated. The victorious Celts then marched on to Rome where they looted the city.

AN END TO EXPANSION

By around 300 B.C. the Romans had grown powerful enough to prevent the Celts from expanding their Italian territory any farther south. The Celts were also being resisted by the Greeks. In the winter of 279 B.C., Celts and Greeks confronted each other at the site of the Oracle at Delphi, where Celts plundered the sacred temple. With the help of bad weather and landslides, the Greeks eventually defeated the Celts and forced them to retreat from Greece.

THE DECLINE OF THE CELTS

Celtic power probably reached its peak in the second century B.C. By that time, however, other peoples were becoming more powerful and the Celts found themselves threatened on three frontiers. In the north they were harassed by the Germanic tribes, and in the east they were attacked by the Dacians. From the south, the Roman legions marched relentlessly onward. By the first century A.D., only Britain and Ireland would remain as truly Celtic countries.

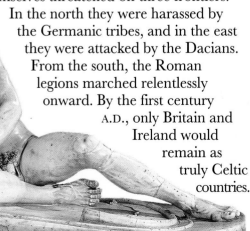

We know a lot about what the Celts looked like from Roman statues like this one, called the Dying Gaul. *In spite of its title, it shows one of the Celts who settled in Galatia.*

CLOTHES AND APPEARANCE

A wealthy Celtic couple dressed for a feast. The woman is fastening the man's cloak with a brooch. Called a penannular brooch, it had a pin that went through the material, then the top was twisted around to hold it in place.

The Celts wore clothing made to keep them warm, rather than fashionable. This meant that their style of dress did not alter very much over the centuries. In spite of this, we know that the Celts were proud of their appearance and took care to maintain their looks. According to the Greek geographer Strabo, fines were levied on those who became too fat to buckle their belts!

CLOTHING

Men dressed in long wool trousers, called *bracae*, and wore shoes or ankle boots made from soft leather. When the weather was warm, they wore close-fitting sleeveless shirts, fastened in the front with brooches or clasps. When it was cold, however, they wore long-sleeved wool tunics that were drawn in at the waist with a belt. In really cold weather, they also wore heavy wool cloaks.

Celtic women dressed simply, in long, loose-fitting gowns made from wool cloth. These were gathered at the waist with a belt, which was usually made from cloth or leather and fastened with a buckle. They draped shawls around their shoulders in cool weather and wore cloaks when it was very cold. Like the men, they usually wore shoes made from leather. Some women must have worn sandals or gone barefoot, as toe-rings have been found on some skeletons.

Celts checked their appearance in bronze mirrors like this one found in England. The back is richly engraved with a pattern that was probably drawn with a compass. The other side is smooth and highly polished to give a clear reflection.

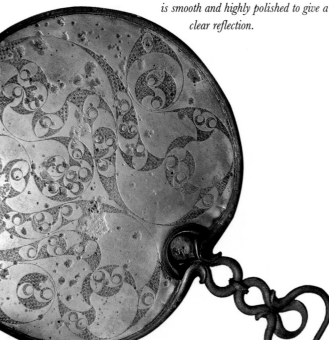

JEWELRY

The Celts did not have zippers or buttons, so they used pins and brooches to fasten their clothing. The most common brooches were called *fibulae* and were shaped somewhat like a modern safety pin. Some were plain; others were made of gold or silver and might be decorated with coral or enamel. The Celts loved finery, and both men and women adorned themselves with bracelets and rings. Women also wore glass or metal beads around their necks.

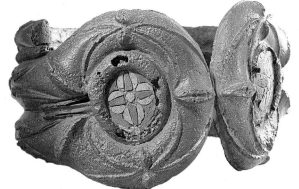

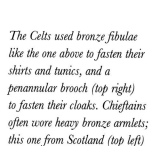

MEN'S HAIRSTYLES

We know from a Greek writer, Diodorus Siculus, that Celtic men were particular about their hair. They had razors for shaving, and used rather clumsy, shearlike scissors to trim their mustaches, of which they were very proud.

Some of them shave the beard, but others let it grow a little; and the nobles shave their cheeks, but they let the mustache grow until it covers the mouth.

Diodorus Siculus

Celtic men preferred to have fair hair. If a Celtic man was born with dark hair, he might wash it in limewater (a mixture of limestone and water) to lighten it. Some Celtic men also used limewater to stiffen their hair until it stood straight up. Without doubt, this would have added to their frightening appearance in battle!

NEW CLOTHES

Unlike us, the Celts could not go shopping when they wanted new clothes. Instead, they had to make their own. They also had to make their own cloth, first by shearing the wool from their sheep and then by spinning it into yarn, using a spindle and whorl. To achieve the bright colors and striped and checked fabrics they liked, the yarn was dyed using vegetable dyes from plants such as woad, madder, and weld.

WORKING THE LOOM

Women then wove the yarn into cloth using an upright loom with a wooden frame. Because they had to "throw" (weave) the shuttle from one side of the loom to the other by hand, the width of their cloth was only as wide as their arm span. They could weave to whatever length they needed, however, before taking the cloth from the loom. They would then cut it out and sew it with a bone needle.

The Celts used bronze fibulae like the one above to fasten their shirts and tunics, and a penannular brooch (top right) to fasten their cloaks. Chieftains often wore heavy bronze armlets; this one from Scotland (top left) is decorated with enamel and colored glass.

A Celtic mustache and a torc (neck-ring) show up well on this carving found in the Czech Republic. The man is probably a noble.

Spinning and weaving were time-consuming activities. Women spent time doing both every day. If the weather was fine, they worked outside where it was easier to see what they were doing.

9

SOCIETY AND GOVERNMENT

A gold torc worn around his neck showed that a man was a warrior or a noble.

Learned men were often asked to help settle tribal disputes. Some disputes, however, were settled by a fight to the death.

Although the Celts dominated much of Europe, they never had an empire and were never united under one ruler. Instead, they were divided up into different tribes in different areas. Each tribe had its own leader. Often several tribes would join together to fight against a common enemy, but they were equally likely to fight among themselves.

SOCIAL GROUPS

All the Celtic tribes were organized along similar lines, no matter where they lived. Celtic society was divided into four main groups: nobles, warriors, farmers, and learned men.

RULERS

At the top of society were the rulers, who came from either the noble or the warrior class. They might have inherited their titles from their fathers, but in some tribes rulers were nominated by a council of nobles. A ruler's claim to power was probably precarious, and often challenged by ambitious noblemen.

Celtic rulers were usually men, but women also played important roles in leadership. Some noblewomen became rulers of their tribes and even went to war! At the time of the Roman conquest of Britain, the Brigantes tribe in the north of England was ruled by Queen Cartimandua, while in A.D. 60, Boadicea, or Boudicca, became queen of the Iceni tribe in eastern England after the death of her husband.

This 19th-century statue of Queen Boadicea in her war chariot stands beside the Thames River in London.

LOOKING AFTER THE SICK

The Celts were superstitious and probably saw sickness as a punishment from their gods. Sometimes they made sacrifices to placate the gods and assist in the patient's recovery. Despite this belief, the Celts tried their best to treat diseases and injuries themselves. Doctors prepared medicines and ointments from herbs, and some performed operations. These might include resetting broken bones or even boring into a patient's skull to relieve pressure on the brain after a serious injury. Unfortunately, the Celts had no antiseptics or painkillers other than alcohol and a few herbs, so patients rarely would have survived such an operation. As early as 300 B.C. some of the tribes in Ireland ran primitive hospitals where the old and the sick could be looked after.

The Celts suffered injuries in accidents as well as in battle. This man's head wound is being tended by a learned man who is skilled in healing.

FARMERS AND LEARNED MEN

Farmers made up the largest group in Celtic society, since nearly everybody needed to farm some land in order to eat. Many farmers were also part-time warriors, while the wealthiest among them might also be nobles. Learned men probably did some farming, too, but most of their time was devoted to other work. They might be doctors, Druids (holy men), metalworkers, or bards or poets. A tribe's bard or poet would have the job of learning the tribe's history and passing it on to the next generation. Learned men were depended on to keep things running smoothly in their tribe.

A CARING SOCIETY

In spite of their love of war and fighting, the Celts lived in a society that cared about the elderly and the infirm. People who were too old or too ill to care for themselves were usually looked after by younger members of their families. If they had no relations, however, neighbors and friends tried to make them as comfortable as possible by ensuring that they had enough food and heat, as well as adequate clothing and shelter.

MINING AND METALWORK

Celts who mined for salt used tools made from stone, wood, or bronze (above) because the salt they were digging out would have rusted iron tools. There was no explosive gas in salt mines, so they could use an uncovered flame for light. Even so, conditions must have been dark, cramped, and miserable.

The Celts owed a lot of their wealth to two related skills. These were mining and metalworking, in both of which they excelled. They mined metal, as well as salt.

MINING FOR SALT

Celtic farmers could never grow enough fodder to feed all their farm animals over the winter. So at the end of the autumn, they slaughtered the animals that were not needed for breeding the following year. The meat was then used to feed the farmer and his family throughout the winter.

Because there were no refrigerators or freezers, the only way to keep meat from going bad was to preserve it with salt. People who lived near the coast could obtain their salt by collecting sea water in salt-pans and letting it evaporate until only the salt crystals remained.

For people living inland, finding salt was much more difficult. However, in the mountains around Hallstatt there was good-quality salt underground. The miners began by making sloping shafts in the mountainside. Next they dug tunnels into the salt using picks. It was a difficult and very dangerous job, but the Celts of Hallstatt were able to mine enough salt to supply all their own needs and still have enough to trade with their neighbors.

MINING FOR COPPER

The Celts in central Europe also mined for copper ore, which could be smelted and turned into metal quite easily. However, copper on its own is quite soft, so it is usually mixed with tin to make a metal called bronze. In early Celtic times, most bronze tools and weapons had been replaced by stronger iron ones, so bronze was used mainly to decorate weapons and to make jewelry and household utensils.

The Gundestrup Cauldron from Denmark is a fine example of Celtic metalworking skills. It is made in silver and gilt and embossed (molded) with figures both inside and out.

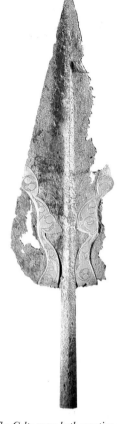

CASTING BRONZE

By Celtic times, bronzesmiths knew how to cast molten bronze into ingots, small bars that could be hammered into bronze sheets of various thicknesses. They also knew how to cast bronze into molds made from stone, clay, or bone, to make all sorts of small objects.

DIGGING FOR IRON

The iron from which the Celts made tools and weapons comes from iron ore. Iron ore was more plentiful than copper ore and was also much easier for the Celts to obtain. It was often found in nodules, or lumps, in marshy or wooded areas. This meant it could be dug out of the ground without using complicated mining techniques. The iron ore was then placed in a small, bowl-shaped furnace. In order to smelt the ore, the charcoal fire in the furnace had to be kept very hot. When it was hot enough, a bloom, or lump, of purer iron formed in the bottom of the furnace.

Celtic blacksmiths made ornamental items for the homes of the wealthy in addition to tools and weapons. This one is making a firedog, a stout framework in which a fire can be contained. The piece on the anvil would be finished off in the shape of an animal's head.

THE BLACKSMITH'S FORGE

Iron was more difficult to work with than bronze, because it would not melt properly at the temperatures the Celts could achieve in their simple furnaces. The bloom of iron that was smelted out of the ore was too stiff to pour into molds. In order to make objects from it, it had to be forged by the blacksmith. To do this, he held the bloom of iron in long-handled tongs over his fire until the iron glowed red-hot. He then started to hammer it on his anvil into the shape he wanted. Once the iron began to cool, the smith stopped hammering and held it back over the fire until it was red-hot. He could then shape it until it cooled down again. This process of shaping and reheating was repeated until he had completed the object.

The Celts were both creative and practical. The bronze design on this iron spearhead is just for decoration, while the bronze bands on the wooden bucket (below) serve a useful purpose; they hold the wooden staves together and stop the bucket from leaking.

In Spain, the Celts built many of their houses with stone walls, so the remains of some of them can still be seen today. These ones are at Castro de Coaña, in Asturias. As you can see, the houses were round in shape and stood near the top of a hill.

Daily life for most Celts centered on the home. At first, most lived in isolated farmsteads with their families. But as some Celts grew rich through trading or mining, they built forts to protect themselves. Later, communities grew up that developed into fortified towns and villages.

HILL FORTS

The Celts built their forts on the top of hills, which not only made them easy to defend, but also gave them a good view of the surrounding countryside. The earliest Celtic hill forts date from between 800 and 600 B.C. and are found in the area immediately north of the Alps. By 600 B.C., hill forts were being built in what is now eastern France and southwest Germany.

In Britain, hill forts existed as early as 1000 B.C., before the arrival of the Celts. Both then and in early Celtic times hill forts seem to have served a different purpose from many of those in mainland Europe. Instead of being the homes of wealthy traders or princes, they were places where a local tribe could gather in times of danger. Later, some of the hill forts might have housed religious centers, where the tribe could meet for ceremonies. Others developed into fortified villages. It must have taken the Celts months to build the protective banks that surrounded their settlements, since all the soil had to be dug out with shovels and piled up without the help of any machinery.

OPPIDA

The settlements known as *oppida* were the Celtic equivalent of our towns and villages. Most of them were marketplaces, and some developed into important trading centers. Although some of them were surrounded by earthworks, they were not as well defended as the hill forts. By the first century B.C., many oppida had paved roads and drainage systems, probably copied from Roman towns that Celtic traders had visited.

Although this settlement is small, it is protected by ditches and banks, topped by a sturdy fence. The only way in and out was through the gates where an enemy could easily be seen and defeated. In peaceful times, the fence also kept the farm animals in—or out.

14

THE FAMILY

An oppidum might have contained any number of houses. These were occupied not just by a man, his wife, and children, but by a large extended family. This could include any of the man's unmarried brothers or sisters until they had homes and families of their own. Elderly parents might also live with one of their married children, as might any unmarried uncles or aunts. Members of the family were very supportive of each other and put kinship ties above loyalty to their tribe.

HOUSEWORK

The Celts did not have many labor-saving devices, so a lot of their time was taken up with keeping the family clothed and fed. Much of this work was done by the women, but the men probably helped when they were not too busy with the farmwork. One job that had to be done frequently was grinding grain into flour to make bread. This was done by hand on a stone *quern*, or mill. In the earliest of these, the grain was placed on a large, flat stone and ground into flour by rubbing a smaller stone backward and forward over it. Using this method could take almost an hour to produce just one pound of flour! After the second century B.C., however, the invention of the rotating quern sped up the process and a pound of flour could be produced in about five minutes.

CHILDREN

There were no schools in Celtic times. Children were at home all day. They probably learned to do things by watching their parents and other family members until they were old enough to help with simple jobs in the house and on the farm. These might include weeding the crops and scaring the birds away, or helping to comb the tangles out of the wool before it was spun into yarn. Celtic children probably also found time to play with simple dolls and models of animals. Young boys also played sports such as hurling, a game resembling field hockey.

Games of chance seem to have been popular as colored glass counters have been found at some excavations. Unfortunately no sets of rules exist now, so we do not know how the games were played.

In this scene inside a Celtic house, the woman on the right is using a rotating quern to grind grain into flour, while the woman on the left is shaping dough into loaves. These would then be baked in the beehive-shaped oven in the background or on a heated stone slab on the hearth.

15

HOUSE AND HOME

In the see-through scene below we can see buildings in a Celtic settlement like those in Gaul (France). Some of the villagers are building a new grain storehouse on the left—perhaps rain has been seeping into the grain pit and making the grain moldy. In the pool of water (bottom right), some villagers are mixing mud or clay to daub on the grain storehouse's wattle panels.

Celtic family homes in Britain, Spain, and Portugal were often round in shape, but in other parts of Europe they were square or oblong. Most of them had a steeply sloping roof of straw or reeds, called a thatched roof. This was so that rain or snow would run off quickly, rather than soaking through and causing the roof to collapse. The walls were built with whatever materials were available locally. In some areas stone was used, but wood was more common. The wood might be made into planks or a frame to support wattle-and-daub (mud plastered on woven sticks).

INSIDE THE HOUSE

Celtic houses had one common room in which everybody ate, slept, cooked, and did their daily chores. There was probably very little furniture; ancient writers tell us that the Celts sat on animal skins. These were either spread out on the floor, which was made of hard-packed earth, or on a bench built along the wall where people slept at night. The hearth with its fire was the most important feature of a Celtic home. It provided heat for cooking and also gave off light, which was essential, as the houses did not have windows. However, the fire also made the house dirty because there were no chimneys and soot often fell back inside if the smoke could not escape through gaps in the thatched roof.

OUTBUILDINGS

Some Celts built a shelter for their animals and a storeroom for the hay that they fed to them. They probably also had a shelter for their plows, their tools, and any farm carts or chariots they owned. They also had special buildings in which grain could be stored in sacks for a short period. Unlike the other buildings, these had wood-planked floors and were raised above the ground on legs to prevent rats and mice from getting in and eating the grain. The Celts also stored some of their grain in pits that were about six feet deep and were lined with wicker or stone. Once they were filled with grain, the pits were sealed with clay to keep the air out.

1 **Timber frame**
2 **Wattle-and-daub walls**
3 **Thatched roof**
4 **Hearth**
5 **Packed-earth sleeping platform**
6 **Grain storehouse**
7 **Constructing a grain storehouse**

HARD WORK

The Celts had no power tools to help them, so building a house must have been very hard work. The right sort of timber had to be cut down in the forest and brought back to the site. It was then trimmed into shape to make the frame. Holes were dug for the upright posts, and the main timbers were strapped into position. Meanwhile, reeds or straw had been cut and dried for the thatched roof. The walls were filled in with wattle-and-daub panels. These were made by weaving together long, thin twigs and plastering them with thick mud.

Twenty years later, the house would probably have to be rebuilt because all the materials would be rotting.

8 **Grain storage pit**
9 **Protective earth rampart and ditch**
10 **Wooden palisade (stake fence)**

Celtic houses had thick thatched roofs to keep out the rain and the wind. They do not seem to have had smoke-holes or chimneys, but perhaps the smoke slowly worked its way through the woven reeds. You can lift the see-through page to see inside the house. There are very few furnishings—just a hearth and a raised platform for sleeping.

FOOD AND FARMING

A Celtic farmer's tools, such as these sheepshears and sickle, were very much like those still used by farmers at the start of the 20th century.

Farming was very important to the Celts, no matter where they lived. This was because each family had to grow all its own food. It was difficult work, since Celtic farmers did not have the many aids such as chemical fertilizers and machinery that we rely on today.

PLOWING THE FIELDS

Like all their other farming tools, the Celts' plow was better than any that had been used before in central and northern Europe. Although it was still made mostly from wood, it had an iron tip that not only made the plow stronger, but also could be easily replaced. Celtic plows could not turn the soil or dig very deeply, however, so they were only useful where the soil was light and easy to work.

Because of this, Celtic farmers preferred to farm in upland areas, rather than in the valley bottoms where the soil was heavier. To break up the soil more thoroughly, the fields were probably plowed twice, the second time at a right angle to the first. Large stones were pulled out and thrown to the side, where they eventually formed boundaries between fields. These can still be seen today in parts of Britain and Ireland.

CROPS

Like farmers today, the Celts planted grain crops such as rye, wheat, barley, and oats. They also grew vegetables such as beans and lentils, which could be stored over the winter and eaten when other food was scarce. Some fields were reserved as pastures, or used for growing grass. Grass was cut in the summer and dried to make hay to feed livestock over the winter.

At least two people were needed to plow a field: one to guide the ox team, and the other to guide the plow. Other people were kept busy picking out the stones the plow turned up and driving the cattle away from the newly plowed area.

SEED, BREAD, AND BEER

In Celtic times crops did not produce as many seeds or grains as their equivalents do now, so large amounts had to be harvested to provide all of a family's needs. The whole family probably helped with the harvesting. The crops were then taken back to the farm buildings to be threshed by hand. This removed the chaff (husks) and left a pile of grain.

Some of the grain had to be saved as seed for planting the next year's crop. The rest of it was stored in grain pits until it was needed. Most of the stored grain would be ground into flour for bread or meal for porridge and stews, but some of it was used to brew beer.

FARM ANIMALS

As well as growing crops, the Celts kept animals on their farms. These were early breeds of the animals you would expect to see on farms today. They included pigs, which were kept for their meat; cattle, which provided meat, milk, and leather; and sheep, which provided milk and wool. As sheep were kept primarily for their wool, they were not killed until they were old—by which time their meat would be too tough to eat. Hens and geese were kept for their eggs and feathers, but it was against the law to eat their flesh. The Celts probably also kept swarms of bees in wicker hives to provide them with honey, which was the only sweetener available in ancient times.

HUNTING

The Celts also enjoyed hunting the fierce animals that roamed the woods and forests surrounding their farms. Their favorite was the wild boar, which they liked to eat, but they also hunted wolves and other animals that might eat their flocks and crops. They usually killed the animals with long-handled spears but sometimes they used iron-tipped arrows or even slingshots.

As you can see from this bronze model from Spain, the Celts rode on horseback when they went hunting. The bell on the horse's neck would perhaps frighten the boar out of hiding, and the dog would chase it until it was tired and easier to catch.

Old grain pits were filled in with trash. This often included items such as cracked pots and broken tools, which provide archaeologists with valuable evidence of Celtic life. In the background some men are unloading freshly cut timber.

19

FEASTS AND CELEBRATIONS

Decorated flagons (bottles), like this one found in France, were used to serve wine at a rich man's feast.

Feasts and celebrations were the highlights of the Celtic year. They were usually rowdy, often extravagant affairs at which the Celts could indulge their love of eating and drinking. At large feasts the whole tribe could meet to display their unity and loyalty to their chieftain. Some feasts were held to celebrate special festivals in the Celtic year, such as the New Year. Others were held just to bring people together, the same as we might throw a party just to have a good time.

SPECIAL FOOD AND DRINK

Alcohol played an important part at feasts. Wine was imported from Italy by those who could afford it, but poorer people drank mead, a honey wine, or beer brewed from wheat and perhaps sweetened with honey. Sometimes the drink was served in a cup that a slave or young boy carried from one person to the next. The men were said to drink only a little at a time from this cup, but they were also said to do it frequently and were well-known for their drunkenness!

The Celts enjoyed eating meat at their feasts. Meat was either roasted on a spit or stewed in a huge cauldron with herbs and vegetables. There might be pork, beef, wild boar, venison, and anything else the hunters had caught. The bravest warrior expected the best cut of meat and might start a fight if he didn't get it.

Celtic feasts were colorful, as well as noisy, with everyone dressed in their best clothes and jewelry. At this feast, the bard is telling a story, while a man in the background is playing music on a type of early flute. The person on the left is serving wine imported from the Romans.

20

The priests, or Druids, played a large part in all the Celtic festivals. At Beltane they supervised the building of the bonfires and the driving of the cattle between them. From comments made by the Romans, we know that they often wore white robes on these occasions.

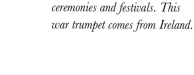

The harsh cry of Celtic trumpets and great horns probably announced the beginning of ceremonies and festivals. This war trumpet comes from Ireland.

HOSPITABLE HOSTS

The Celts were hospitable and often welcomed strangers at their feasts. The writer Diodorus Siculus reported, "They also invite strangers to their banquets, and only after the meal do they ask who they are and of what they stand in need." As well as being fed, guests would be entertained by the tribe's bard with stories of the tribe's past glories. Boasting contests might also develop between warriors eager to brag of their prowess.

SAMHAIN

The Celts divided their year into four parts, and the beginning of each part was marked by a festival. *Samhain* was the name for the festival of the New Year. It was celebrated on November 1, when the animals were brought in from grazing and those not needed for breeding were slaughtered for food. Because Samhain fell between the old and the new year, it was thought to be a time of magic, when armies of magical soldiers marched out from caves and mounds in the earth, and people and spirits could mingle in each other's worlds. In Christian times, Samhain was replaced by All Saints' Day, or All Hallows' Day. The day before it became known as Halloween. Some of the old Celtic beliefs still linger in traditional Halloween celebrations.

BELTANE, IMBOLC, AND LUGNASAD

Beltane was celebrated at the beginning of May. It marked the time when the cattle were sent out to graze in the open again after being sheltered and fed near the farmhouse all winter. As part of the celebrations, the Celts lit huge bonfires and drove their cattle between them. They believed that this would protect the cattle from diseases.

Imbolc, on February 1, was dedicated to the Celtic goddess Brigit. It was celebrated as the start of the lambing season when the ewes' milk was plentiful again. This was important not only for nursing the lambs, but also for making cheese.

Lugnasad, on August 1, was celebrated as the time when the crops began to ripen in the fields, giving the promise of a good harvest and plenty to eat over the coming winter. It was a day sacred to the powerful Celtic god Lugh, also known as Lugos.

This cauldron, called a krater, would be filled with wine at a feast. It was made of bronze and would hold many quarts.

21

RELIGION AND RITUAL

The Celts had many gods and goddesses. Some were worshipped by all Celts, while many tribes had their own special gods. There were gods of warfare and hunting, and goddesses of fertility, healing, and good harvests.

GODS OF NATURE

Most Celts were farmers who relied heavily on the seasons and the forces of nature for their survival, so their religion was closely related to their natural surroundings. Many of their gods and goddesses were associated with trees, stones, lakes, and springs. Over all of these deities reigned the Earth Mother. Each tribe also had its own tribal god. It was believed that all gods and goddesses demanded respect, and so offerings and sacrifices were sometimes made to them.

To make sacrifices to their gods, the priests threw valuable items such as gold cups and weapons into the water. The blades of swords, knives, and daggers were often bent or broken before they were thrown in.

HOLY WELLS AND SPRINGS

The Celts relied on natural wells and springs as a source of drinking water for themselves and their animals. Because water came from the earth, it was associated with the Earth Mother, so most of the wells and springs were thought to be the homes of goddesses, rather than gods.

The Celts believed that the water goddesses had the power to make sick people well, to protect people in battle, or to prevent a particular spring from drying up in a drought. If a Celt wanted to ask a favor of a water goddess, he or she might make a sacrifice to the goddess by throwing some of his or her most valued possessions into the water.

One of the most important of the water goddesses was Elen, who was also a goddess of healing. Another was Sulis, who guarded the hot springs at Bath, England. When the Romans later built a town on the site, they named it after her, calling it Aquae Sulis, meaning "Waters of Sulis."

SACRED GROVES

Certain groves of trees were as sacred to the Celts as churches or temples are to us. According to the Roman poet Lucan, the Celts let the sacred groves grow wild so that the branches of the trees met overhead and blocked out the sunlight. Within these groves were images of the gods that were roughly carved from tree-trunks. There were also altars on which the Druids, or priests, performed sacrifices. These might have been animal or even human sacrifices, as Lucan said the trees were sprinkled with human blood.

THE DRUIDS

Religious ceremonies and sacrifices were performed by the tribe's priests. In Britain and Gaul the priests were known as Druids and probably came from noble families. The Druids were also teachers and versed in the laws of the tribe. Sometimes they even made decisions about whether the tribe should go to war or not. Many of their rituals were performed in secret. They never wrote anything down and they also forbade other people to read or write. Their knowledge was passed down by word of mouth and it could take up to 20 years for a novice to acquire all the knowledge he needed to become a Druid.

Many carvings and statues of Celtic gods have been found. Above you can see three different images of the water goddess Coventina. The statue on the left is of the Dagda, or Good God, of Ireland.

OAK TREES AND MISTLETOE

To the Celts, the oak was the most sacred tree. Mistletoe was thought to be sacred, too, and was believed to aid healing and encourage fertility.

They believe that the mistletoe, taken in drink, imparts fertility to barren animals, and that it is an antidote for all poisons.

—— Pliny ——

However, the Druids were also probably aware of mistletoe's poisonous properties, as its juice was drunk by sacrificial victims.

Only Druids were allowed to enter the sacred groves where the mistletoe grew. They cut it with a golden sickle during a specific phase of the moon and caught it on a white cloth so that it did not touch the ground.

One of a priest's tasks was probably to put together a calendar for the year. This one, found in France, shows lucky and unlucky days.

23

DEATH AND BURIAL

The early Celts believed that there was a life after death. They thought that when a person died, he or she went to a place known as the "Otherworld" where life went on much the same as before. After a time, a person would die in the Otherworld and be reborn in this one. This meant that people might be reunited with their families and friends time after time.

When you turn over the see-through page you will see inside the tomb of a noblewoman found beneath a stone cairn at Vix in France. She had been placed on a wagon, along with pottery such as this decorated cup from Greece (right). On the right you can also see part of the decorated rim of the huge Greek bronze krater, or cauldron, that was buried with her.

GRAVE GOODS

The Celts often buried some of a dead person's favorite belongings with the body. These might be their best clothes and other objects that would be useful in the next world. The Celts also buried things that the person might need on the journey to the Otherworld, such as food and drink. Joints of pork were a favorite, and one man was buried with 9 gallons of Italian wine.

1 Noblewoman wearing torc
2 Wagon
3 Wheels from wagon
4 The Vix krater
5 The Hochdorf prince
6 Bronze couch
7 Drinking horns
8 Bronze dishes on wagon
9 Bronze cauldron from Italy
10 Flowers

CREMATIONS

Some Celts cremated their dead, rather than burying the bodies. After the cremation, the remains of the bones were put into a pot or an urn and this was buried in a small grave. Even these graves often contained food and drink and other items that might be useful in the Otherworld. In some regions very few Celtic burials have been found — perhaps in these regions the Celts simply scattered the ashes of their dead.

CHARIOT BURIALS

Chariots were as important to the Celts in death as they were in life. In addition to transporting the dead person to their grave, a chariot was often also buried with the body. Some chariots were taken apart. The wheels were then laid on their sides in the bottom of the grave and the body was placed on top of them. Others were left standing upright and in one piece. In one case, two horses were buried as well!

No one is sure whether these chariots were supposed to take the dead person on the journey to the Otherworld or whether they were a mark of a person's high standing in this one.

PRINCELY TOMBS

This name is given to many spectacular graves found mainly in parts of Germany and France. As you can see from the picture below, they look like large grassy mounds sticking up in the landscape. Unfortunately, because the mounds were so visible, they later became easy targets for grave-robbers who stole much of the gold and other treasures that had been buried with the dead.

The scene below shows early Celts building a mound, or tumulus, over the tomb of a prince. The Hochdorf prince, who is shown under the see-through page, was buried beneath a mound like this.

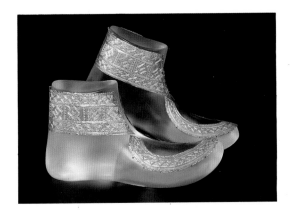

Lift up the see-through page below to see inside the tomb of a Celtic prince. He was buried in about 525 B.C. at Hochdorf in what is now Germany. His wooden burial chamber was built in a pit, then a mound nearly 20 feet high and 200 feet in diameter was piled above him. On the left is one of the bronze lions that decorate a huge cauldron found in his tomb. When you lift the see-through scene you will see that the prince must have been wearing shoes decorated with gold when he was buried. The rest of the shoes rotted away, but these gold bands were found on his feet.

CRAFTWORKERS

Most Celtic families were self-sufficient and could produce their own food and clothes, and make the utensils and simple tools they needed for daily life. If a Celt wanted something special, however, and could afford it, he or she would visit a craftworker who made a living from producing fine objects.

AMAZING ARTISTRY

The artistry of Celtic craftsmen was renowned in the ancient world. But when archaeologists first discovered beautifully made objects on Celtic sites, they thought the Celts must have imported them from other peoples such as the Greeks or the Romans. They could not believe that the Celts had the skills needed to produce such fine workmanship in glass, enamel, gold, and bronze, as well as in silver, iron, and wood. But gradually archaeologists began to find evidence, such as special molds, tools, and waste products, showing that the Celts had indeed made many of these objects themselves.

THE GOLDSMITH

Gold was the Celts' favorite metal for jewelry and decoration. To make jewelry such as the torcs, or neck-rings, the goldsmith first stretched out the gold to make thin strands of wire. These were then twisted together into what looked like a golden rope. This was bent into shape to fit around the warrior's neck and the two ends were completed with an ornamental end of gold, called a finial. The patterns on these were formed in a decorated mold.

If the goldsmith wanted to decorate an object such as a special pair of shoes, he would first shape the gold into small bars, or ingots. The ingots were then hammered out into a large, flat sheet that could be cut out into a delicate pattern or stamped with a patterned die.

Many of the Celts' favorite designs were based on circles. A pair of iron compasses was used to scratch the outline of the design onto the metal of the object to be decorated. The shapes could then be cut out to make an openwork pattern or filled in with colored enamel.

GLASSWARE

By about 250 B.C. the Celts in central Europe had discovered how to make glass. They could only make it in very small amounts and so could not use it for any large objects such as windows for their houses. Instead, they used it to make ornaments and jewelry such as beads and bracelets. The Celts were particularly fond of colored glass. They produced different colors by adding different minerals, such as powdered copper and iron, to the glass while it was still molten or liquid. Once a bead or a bracelet had been made, patterns could be added to it by trailing small amounts of different colored liquid glass onto it. Some patterns were also molded on while the bracelets and beads were being made.

WORKING WITH ENAMEL

The Celts liked to decorate their bronzeware with enamel. They often used their favorite color, bright red, but yellow, blue, and green enamels were also popular. To make the enamel, Celtic enamelers heated a mixture of quartz glass, lead ore, and a mineral such as cuprite at a high temperature in a stone or clay crucible. The enameler then took the object he wanted to decorate and roughened the surfaces that were to be enameled. Next he poured the hot liquid enamel onto the object. As it cooled, it stuck firmly to the roughened surfaces. If more than one color of enamel was wanted on a particular object, the enameler needed a very steady hand to make sure the second color went into the right part of the pattern.

CELTIC DESIGN

Some of the distinctive designs on our jewelry today were originally created by Celtic craftsmen. Many of these designs were based on circles, which Celtic craftsmen made with iron compasses. Swirling knotwork patterns and the three-legged *triskele*, which is still used today as the emblem of the Isle of Man, were also popular. Another favorite was the animal motif. From the number of glass and metal animals that have been found, we know that animal ornaments were popular.

Here are some of the items made by Celtic craftworkers. Most of them are made from bronze and decorated with enamel or with delicate filigree patterns, but the helmet also contains some silver and is decorated with coral.

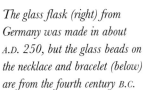

The glass flask (right) from Germany was made in about A.D. 250, but the glass beads on the necklace and bracelet (below) are from the fourth century B.C.

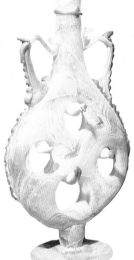

27

TRADE

From the earliest times, the Celts traded with each other and with their neighbors. They traveled long distances to exchange any surplus goods or raw materials for things that they could not produce themselves. Because their civilization lasted for so many centuries and covered such a wide area, the Celts' trading partners included the Phoenicians and the Carthaginians, as well as the Etruscans, the Greeks, and the Romans. These peoples also traded with other peoples, which meant that the Celts could obtain items from all parts of the ancient world, even from countries as far away as China.

SALT, TIN, AND COPPER

The earliest recorded Celtic traders were those who took salt over the Alps from their mines around Hallstatt to the cities of Greece. There must have been traders before these, however, as tin and copper—the two metals needed to make bronze—were not found in all parts of Europe. Copper was more widely available, but tin was only found in Cornwall (in England), Brittany (in France), and northwest Spain and Portugal. To reach bronzesmiths in other parts of Europe, traders had to transport the tin long distances over land. They might even have had to cross the sea.

BARTER OR CASH?

For many centuries, the Celts bartered for the goods they wanted rather than paying for them with money. They also paid for goods by giving the seller their value in iron bars. In later Celtic times, coins came into widespread use, so the Celts were able to pay for goods with them. The first coins used by the Celts were brought from Greece by Celtic mercenary soldiers.

LUXURY GOODS

Although the Celts were able to produce many beautiful objects themselves, rich Celts often imported luxury goods to enhance their status in the community. At first these goods were laboriously carried over the mountains by Celtic traders. By about 600 B.C., however, the Greeks had established a trading colony called Massilia near the mouth of the Rhône river. Massilia gave Celtic traders access by sea to other Mediterranean ports and along the river valleys to most of the western Celtic lands.

This made the transport of goods much easier. Many of the luxurious objects that have been found in Celtic burial grounds in France, Germany, and Switzerland must have traveled along these routes.

Iron bars like these have been found on Celtic sites. About 30 inches long, they were probably used as currency, but could also have been used to repair iron tools and weapons.

Slaves who had been captured by the Celts were sold to the Romans in exchange for goods such as wine. They often ended up in the slave markets of Rome. There they were sold to the highest bidder, who might well have then taken them to work in an entirely different part of the Roman Empire.

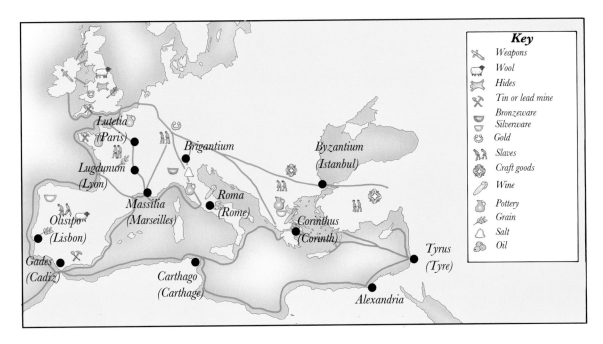

As this map of their trading routes shows, the Celts transported their goods both by land and by sea. Not all the Celts made long journeys. Instead, they might take their goods to one place and exchange goods with a trader from another place, then both parties would return home.

TRADE WITH THE ROMANS

The Celts' most important trading partners were the Romans, especially as the Roman Empire increased in size. To run their empire successfully, the Romans relied heavily on slave labor. Slaves did not just serve in the houses of the rich. They were also put to work on farms, and in mines and other industries. Some slaves were people who had been captured by the Celts and traded to the Romans, often in exchange for fine Italian wine. Because the Celts would accept a single jar of wine for a slave, the Romans felt they were getting the better bargain.

The Romans were especially fond of the wool cloth produced by the Celts. They probably used the checked and striped designs for blankets, but their favorite was plain red cloth from the Celts in Britain.

However, what seemed like an easy trade to the Romans was not necessarily a bad bargain for the Celts. In Celtic society, the possessor of such fine wine was held in high esteem.

CLOTH AND POTTERY

The Romans also bought good-quality wool cloth from the Celts. Though some Romans mocked the Celts as barbarians who dressed in animal skins, Celtic cloth was of far better quality than anything the Romans could produce. In exchange, the Celts took Roman pottery and glassware. A lot of the pottery was bought by the Celts in southern Gaul. They then made cheap imitations of it, and in turn traded these with other Celts who lived farther north.

This pottery from Italy, together with fragments of amphorae (jars) that had contained wine, was found at the site of a Celtic trading settlement on the Rhine river in Basle, Switzerland.

TRANSPORTATION

Though travel in Celtic times was difficult and dangerous, the Celts managed to transport themselves and their goods successfully around much of Europe and the Mediterranean. Sometimes they had to go on foot, but they also traveled by horse, by chariot, and by cart, depending on the terrain. The Celts were also skilled boatbuilders, so Celtic tribes who lived near the water were able to travel by boat.

DANGEROUS JOURNEYS

The Europe inhabited by the first Celts was much more heavily forested than it is today, making it difficult to get around. Many early travelers must have lost their way and died of hunger or exhaustion. Some might also have been attacked and killed by the wild animals that roamed the countryside. Travelers in the high mountains would have had to cope with the bitter cold, since there were few places for them to find shelter. Many of them must have died on these treacherous journeys.

WHEELED TRANSPORTATION

In regions where the ground was not too rough, the Celts often traveled by four-wheeled carts or wagons. Like their chariots, wagons had wooden wheels with iron tires. They were pulled by two horses harnessed to a wooden yoke that was fixed to a central pole. This put a lot of strain on the horses, however, so it was probably not very comfortable for the horses or efficient for the Celts. Though the wagons were useful for families on the move, there were not many smooth roads in Celtic lands, so they were probably only used over short distances.

A trading vessel has arrived in the Celtic port of Geneva. Some Celts in coracles are helping to unload the goods, which others will take away on carts or in smaller boats. Archaeologists have discovered the remains of a 100-foot-long pier with wooden palisades, stakes tied together to form a fence. The pier protected the port from wind and waves.

TRAVELING BY WATER

Many Celts lived alongside rivers or lakes, so boats were important for getting around as well as for fishing. The simplest of these were *coracles*, which are still used today in parts of Wales. Coracles were usually circular, but were sometimes oblong-shaped with rounded corners. They were made of a wickerwork frame with waterproofed animal skins stretched over it and sewn together. They carried one person, who paddled with a single oar. Because they were very light, coracles could easily be lifted out of the water and carried around obstacles, such as rapids or waterfalls.

The Celts used coracles on rivers and lakes, and for short sea journeys. For longer sea journeys the Celts had bigger boats that were made of wood. These could have several pairs of oars and also had a mast so that they could be sailed as well as rowed, depending on what conditions were like on the sea.

SEA JOURNEYS

Traveling by sea was probably even more dangerous for the Celts than traveling into the mountains. They had no charts or maps, and had to rely on the sun and the stars to navigate their way. Even the biggest ships, such as those of the Veneti of western France, could easily be wrecked if a gale suddenly blew up. Because of this, the Celts tried to sail as close to land as possible, and crossed the open sea at its narrowest points.

JOURNEYS IN EASY STAGES

In general the Celts only sailed along parts of the coast that they knew well. When they reached unknown waters they would sail into the nearest harbor and transfer their cargo to another vessel whose crew knew the waters. If the Celts were transporting goods over any long distance by sea, there might be several changes of boat and crew before the cargo reached its final destination.

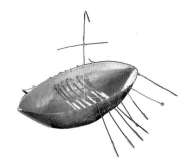

This model of a Celtic ship is made from gold and was found in Ireland. It might have been an offering to the god Manannan mac Lir, king of the ocean.

The Celts believed their port of Geneva (in Switzerland) was protected by a god who is shown in this large oak statue, which dates from around 80 B.C.

A BROCH

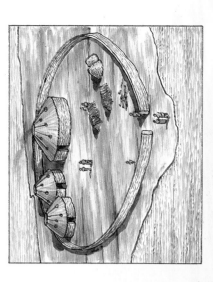

From archaeological evidence we know that most Celtic houses were only one story high. In about the first century B.C., however, Celts living on the north coast of the Scottish mainland and in the Northern and Western Isles began to build tall, round structures known as *brochs*. Built from the local stone, they were about 40 to 80 feet in diameter at the base, but narrower at the top. They were at least 50 feet high and their walls were constructed without using any mortar. Brochs had an inner wall and an outer wall, fastened together in places by long stones. Between the two walls, stone staircases led to the different floors, or galleries.

INSIDE A BROCH

Brochs were built to protect the Celts in times of danger, so the entrance was usually through a single door at ground level. This door led into an open courtyard with a well or hearth in the middle. The living areas were above this on galleries or platforms built out from the inner wall. These galleries had wooden floors and walls. Their roofs sloped down toward the courtyard and were thatched with reeds or straw. More than one family would have sheltered in a broch, so conditions must have been very cramped. It must also have been dark and cold inside, even on a bright day, since the high walls with no windows kept the sun from shining in.

AROUND A BROCH

On the sites of many brochs the remains of other Celtic buildings have been found. These include the houses where the people normally lived and the buildings in which they sheltered their animals and stored their food. There was often also an outer wall to help defend the whole site from enemies. After the end of the first century A.D., it seems that the brochs were abandoned and fell into disrepair. However, many sites remained occupied, and the stones from the brochs were used to make new buildings.

The broch in the see-through scene below is based on one at Clickhimin in Scotland. There had been a settlement on the site for many years before the broch was built (above). Lift up the see-through page to see the settlement with the broch, and inside the broch.

1 **Building guarding outer gateway**
2 **Double stone wall**
3 **Staircase**
4 **Timber gallery**
5 **Thatched roof with stone weights to hold down thatch**
6 **Stone hearth**
7 **Parapet**

Brochs probably evolved from the defensive walls of settlements and forts. People began to build houses and outbuildings against the walls, which in turn became brochs. The tall brochs provided better protection from attackers using fire and slingshots.

wall of fort

broch

buildings inside wall

This picture of the ruins of the broch at Dun Carloway on the Isle of Lewis clearly shows the structure of the double walls with the space for the stairs in between. Over 500 brochs were built in Scotland by the Celts.

HORSEMEN AND CHARIOTEERS

Horses were very important to the Celts. They were not only a means of transportation, but were also ridden for pleasure. There was even a Celtic horse goddess, known as Epona, who was worshipped in Gaul and Britain.

COINS AND CAVALRY

We know that the Celts were very proud of their mounts because horses and chariots are shown on their gold coins from around the first century B.C. The Romans greatly admired the Celts' horsemanship, and recruited many cavalrymen from Celtiberia (Spain) and Gaul into their army.

HORSES AND HARNESSES

Nobody is sure when horses were first ridden in Europe. It is likely that the Celts used them as early as 700 B.C. because large numbers of harness fittings have been found from this time. These include bits for the horse's mouth that are similar to those used by riders today. Enameled harness-mounts, which the Celts used to decorate as well as to strengthen the harness, have also been found. The various leather straps of the harness were linked together by bronze and iron rings. There is no evidence that horses wore shoes, but because the Celts did not ride on paved roads, shoes were not necessary.

Chariot racing was one of the Celts' favorite sports. Chariots were not used in battle after about 200 B.C., except in Britain, but the nobles continued to travel and race in chariots for many years.

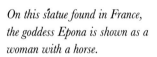

On this statue found in France, the goddess Epona is shown as a woman with a horse.

Archaeologists can learn about Celtic harnesses and chariots by studying coins like this one.

SHOWING OFF

Just as some people today invest a lot of time and money in their cars, the Celts took pride in the way their horses looked. Gold coins show horses with their manes braided and there is evidence that some of them wore caps. Pony caps were worn principally to protect the horse's head from injury. However, it is clear from the fine workmanship of many of these caps that they were also worn for decoration. A pony cap found in Scotland was made from bronze and decorated in a raised pattern of swirls and circles. It had a hole at each side through which the pony's ears would fit and possibly a third hole in between them, which could have held a feathered plume. On another pony cap, tags of metal were attached to the end of streamers, and these would have jangled as the pony moved.

RACING

The Celts were fine horsemen and charioteers who loved to show off their horsemanship. The big races, which were often part of the entertainment at the great feasts, provided the perfect opportunity for the Celts to show off their skills—and for the spectators to gamble on who would win. It is likely that the races also helped young warriors develop the skills they would later need in battle.

A Celtic raiding party might steal cattle and other valuable goods from their neighbors, as well as from their enemies. Raiding also helped the Celts practice their riding and fighting skills.

THE USE OF CHARIOTS

The chariot was the Celts' favorite vehicle. It was lighter and more mobile than a wagon and could even be used on hunting expeditions where the forests were not too thick. When the Celts were at war, however, the chariot was used in battle. Then it held two men. One was the charioteer who held the reins and steered the horses. The other was a warrior who could fight from inside the chariot, or even standing on the front pole to which the horses were yoked. Warriors mostly used chariots to take them into battle, then ran down the pole to fight on foot. If the fight went against them, their charioteer collected them and drove them to safety.

MAKING A CHARIOT

Because wood soon rots in soil, no complete chariots have yet been found. However, we know that they were made of wood and that their wooden wheels had an iron tire that was fitted when it was hot. It would then shrink as it cooled and hold the parts of the wheel firmly together. After the wheels were made and fixed onto their axle, the flat body of the chariot was made and joined to its pole. Panels of wickerwork were then added to the two sides to protect the people in the chariot, but the front was probably left open to make it easier for the warrior to jump out and fight on the pole during a battle.

This Celtic horse bit is similar to those used today. The mold used to make the bit, and a guiding ring, are shown above it.

WARRIORS AND WARFARE

Warriors were very
important people within
Celtic society. Their
courage in battle was highly
respected and they often fought in
other people's armies as well as for
their own tribe. Celtic warriors did
not fear death; to die in battle was
the greatest glory imaginable. To
avoid the dishonor of being taken
prisoner, many warriors committed
suicide.

WEAPONS

Even the poorest warriors had weapons of
some sort. A common weapon was the
spear or javelin, which could be up to
eight feet long. It had an iron head fixed
onto a wooden handle and was probably
thrown at the enemy at the start of a
battle, rather than used like a lance to stab
him. According to Julius Caesar, the Celts
in Gaul also had bows and arrows, while
on several sites in Britain, archaeologists
have found piles of small stones that were
probably used in slingshots.

Wealthier warriors also carried swords.
In early Celtic times, swords had short
blades and were like daggers. These would
only have been really useful for hand-to-
hand fighting. From the third century B.C.,
however, improvements in metalworking
meant that swords could be made much
longer. Using these swords to slash at the
enemy, warriors could also fight from
horseback.

ARMOR

Many Celtic warriors carried a shield to defend themselves in battle. It was usually made of a flat sheet of wood and was often covered with leather to protect it from heavy blows. In shape it was an oval or a rectangle with rounded ends, and could be over four feet tall. The grip, or boss, in the center was often made of iron and could be used as a weapon in hand-to-hand fighting if the shield itself was destroyed. Some Celts protected their heads with helmets made of leather, bronze, or iron. From the third century B.C., a few warriors also wore chainmail shirts to protect their bodies. Chainmail was probably a Celtic invention. Each shirt took a long time to make and was very expensive, so possibly only the most important warriors wore them. In contrast, some Celtic warriors went into battle totally naked, using an herb named woad to paint their bodies blue!

WAR CHARIOTS

The Celts in mainland Europe only used war chariots until the second century B.C., with the last recorded use being at the Battle of Telamon in 225 B.C. Even then, they may well have been used simply as a means of getting the warriors quickly into and out of battle, with all the contact fighting being done on foot. In Britain, however, the Celts rode chariots into battle until at least the first century A.D. They preferred to fight from the chariots, hurling spears at their enemies as they rushed by them at great speed.

CELTIC CAVALRY

It was once thought that Celtic warriors could not have fought properly from horseback because they did not have stirrups (foot-rests) for balance. New evidence has shown, however, that by the third and second centuries B.C. the Celts were using a saddle with four tall pommels. These held the rider firmly in his seat and allowed him to use his thighs for balance. This left his arms free to control the horse and his weapons.

BATTLE TACTICS

Celtic battles seem to have been chaotic affairs. The Celts' armies were often huge, but Celtic soldiers lacked discipline, and they had no real battle plans. Instead, the Celts tried to frighten their enemies into giving up without a fight. First, the most important warriors might try to intimidate their enemies by taunting them. As the taunts were accompanied by fierce war-cries and by the harsh din of the battle trumpets and bagpipes, this tactic must sometimes have proved successful! If it failed, the Celts charged at the enemy at full speed, brandishing spears and swords. If the enemy stood their ground, Celtic warriors would fight to the death, rather than admit defeat.

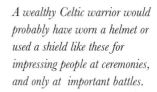

A wealthy Celtic warrior would probably have worn a helmet or used a shield like these for impressing people at ceremonies, and only at important battles.

The Celts thought the head was the most important part of a person's body. If they had the opportunity, they severed the heads from enemies they had killed and took them as trophies. Here a warrior is showing a head to his allies in Hannibal's Carthaginian army.

THE ROMAN CONQUEST

This gold coin from the first century B.C. shows the head of the Gallic chieftain Vercingetorix. After he surrendered to Julius Caesar at Alesia in 52 B.C., he was taken to Rome as a prisoner. In 46 B.C. Caesar paraded him through the streets of the city and then had him executed.

The Celts' victory at the Battle of Allia and sacking of the city of Rome in 390 B.C. were humiliations the Romans could not forget. They were determined to crush the Celts and drive them from their lands.

DEFEAT IN ITALY

By 225 B.C., with an organized and well-equipped army, the Romans were able to put this plan into action. At the Battle of Telamon, the Romans dealt a tremendous blow to their Celtic enemies: 40,000 warriors were killed and at least 10,000 more were taken prisoner. Celtic influence in Italy was destroyed. But this massive defeat was to have even more serious consequences for the Celts, for the Romans realized they could add the Celts' lands to their rapidly growing empire.

This map shows some of the Romans' major victories and conquests in the Celtic lands, and other battles involving the Celts. Many tribes were wiped out completely, but others adopted Roman ways and their warriors even became soldiers in the Roman armies.

ALLIES OF HANNIBAL

The expansionist plans of the Romans were a threat to more people than the Celts. Around 218 B.C., alarmed by Rome's growing might, the Carthaginians of North Africa formed an alliance with some of the Celtic tribes to launch an assault on Rome. Under the leadership of the Carthaginian general, Hannibal, an army set out to march through Spain and Gaul before crossing the Alps into Italy. At the Ticinus river the combined force of Carthaginians and Celts defeated the Romans in battle. But the allies' military success was short-lived. By 202 B.C., the Romans had crushed the Carthaginians and increased their own influence in the Mediterranean region.

CONQUESTS IN GAUL

After defeating the Carthaginians, the Romans turned their attention once again to the conquest of the Celtic lands in Europe. Though the Celts resisted fiercely, they lacked the discipline of the Roman soldiers. By around 60 B.C., Celtic lands in Spain and northern Italy were in Roman hands. Julius Caesar, one of Rome's most distinguished soldiers, was put in charge of the security of two new Roman provinces in northern Italy, Cisalpine and Transalpine Gaul. Caesar was an ambitious man, looking for the chance to gain wealth and glory. He knew that conquering the whole of Gaul would help him achieve his goals.

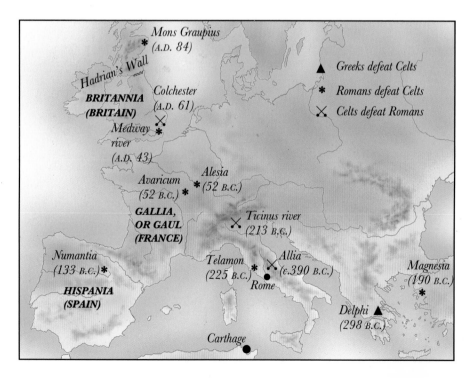

CAESAR'S TRIUMPH

When Caesar's army marched into Gaul, some Celtic tribes were quick to join forces with him. Those that still resisted were treated ruthlessly by the Romans. The Nervii tribe was almost completely destroyed, and the Eburoni tribe was wiped out.

In 52 B.C., under the leadership of Vercingetorix, chieftain of the Averni tribe, the Gallic Celts made a bold attempt to rid their lands of the Romans. Vercingetorix was a clever and courageous leader, but he was eventually trapped by Caesar when he was forced to retreat to the hilltop oppidum of Alesia. There, Caesar promptly laid siege. Although a relief force of 250,000 Celts came to the aid of the besieged Celts, Vercingetorix was forced to surrender. It had been the Gallic Celts' last great stand. Now Gaul, too, became part of the Roman Empire.

BRITAIN

While under Caesar, the Romans made a number of attempts to conquer Britain, but it was not until A.D. 43, in the reign of the Emperor Claudius, that they were finally successful in bringing parts of Britain under Roman rule. Many British Celts resisted the Romans as fiercely as the Celts on mainland Europe had, but others forged alliances with them. As in Gaul, this made it easier for the Romans to subdue Celtic resistance. However, conquest of the north and west proved impossible. Around A.D. 120 the Emperor Hadrian built a northern boundary for the Roman Empire. Known as Hadrian's Wall, the boundary ran from coast to coast. Much of the wall can still be seen today.

This marble statue from Rome shows a Celtic chieftain who has killed his wife and is about to kill himself. Some warriors chose suicide over capture by the enemy.

At the Battle of Telamon an army of around 70,000 Celts was trapped between two Roman armies. The Romans, who were better organized and had superior weapons, heavily defeated the Celts.

THE COMING OF CHRISTIANITY

The see-through scene below shows part of a Celtic Christian monastery. Originally, all of the buildings were made of wood and wattle-and-daub. By the 10th century the main buildings, such as the church and refectory (dining hall), would have been rebuilt in stone. If they were attacked by raiders, such as plundering Vikings, the monks could seek refuge in the stone tower.

Christianity was adopted by the Celts during Roman times. A few Celts had learned about the new religion through their trading links with people from around the Mediterranean. The Romans allowed the vanquished Celts to continue worshipping their old gods, but at first tried to forbid Christianity. They thought it threatened their authority and so the first Christians had to keep their religion secret. Those who were discovered were persecuted.

THE GROWING RELIGION

In spite of this secrecy and persecution, the number of Christians increased, especially among the poor. Then, in A.D. 312, the Roman Emperor Constantine became a Christian after a great victory in battle, and he declared Christianity the religion of the Roman Empire. Although Germanic tribes destroyed Roman power in western Europe, Christianity survived in many regions.

CHRISTIANITY IN BRITAIN

In A.D. 410, the Roman legions left Britain to defend other parts of their empire. At this time, parts of Britain were under threat from the Angles and Saxons who migrated to the south and east coasts in search of new lands to settle. These people brought their own religions to their new homelands, and Christianity became confined to a few followers in the Celtic west of the country, which was untouched by the invaders.

SAINT PATRICK

The most famous Celtic Christian was St. Patrick. The grandson of a Christian priest, Patrick was born on the west coast of Britain around A.D. 385. When he was 16, Patrick was captured by pirates and taken to Ireland. He later escaped to France where he trained as a Christian priest. Around A.D. 432 he returned to Ireland as a bishop. His first attempts to convert the Irish to Christianity met with great opposition, but eventually he was successful. Patrick also persuaded some of his followers to build monasteries.

1 Stone church
2 Altar
3 Wooden lookout tower
4 New stone lookout tower
5 Monks' dining hall, or refectory
6 Souterrain, an underground chamber for storage
7 Brackets holding burning rushes
8 School where monks studied
9 Abbot's house
10 Monk's house, or cell
11 Gatekeeper's house

THE WORK OF THE MONKS

The Christian religion that survived in Ireland and Britain became known as the Celtic Christian Church. By the end of the fifth century, many Celtic Christians had set up monasteries in Wales, England, and France as well as in Ireland.

The monks wanted little to do with politics and worldly affairs. Instead they devoted much time to praying and studying their Bibles. They also looked after the sick and the poor, supporting themselves by farming. Some of the monks left the monasteries to convert other people to Christianity. Others stayed behind to make beautifully decorated copies of religious books. Some of these, such as *The Book of Kells* and the *Lindisfarne Gospels*, can still be seen today.

The Celtic monks lived a simple life, and had very few personal possessions. However, they made and cared for beautiful objects, such as chalices (cups) and books. When the monks copied out manuscripts, they often decorated the pages with designs similar to those used on early Celtic jewelry. In addition to putting patterns on the borders of the page, the monks also made the first letter on a page especially decorative.

MYTHS AND LEGENDS

The Celts loved to tell stories of their tribes, their leaders, and their gods. They also liked to invent stories of imaginary heroes and heroines. These legends were passed from one generation to the next by word of mouth, but many of them have since been lost or forgotten. In Britain and Ireland, however, some of these stories and legends were written down after the decline of the Druids, and can still be read today.

By the 12th century A.D. the legends of King Arthur had spread as far as Italy, but they still contained some strong Celtic elements. For example, after Arthur was mortally wounded in battle, he asked one of his knights to return his sword, Excalibur, to the Lady of the Lake, just as the Celts had sacrificed swords in the past.

KING ARTHUR

Probably the most famous legends from Celtic times are those about King Arthur. These stories were first told in the sixth century A.D., and may have been based on the life of a Welsh chieftain.

The legend of King Arthur became even more popular after the Norman conquest of Britain in 1066, when more stories were added to the old ones. Arthur was then portrayed as a medieval knight and the original story was turned into one of chivalry, courtly love, and romance. Traveling minstrels told the stories throughout Britain, France, and even Italy, and in 1165 Arthur was pictured in a mosaic in Otranto, Italy. At about the same time, the great French poet Chrétien de Troyes wrote several romances about the characters of King Arthur's court. Although these stories were very different from the original Celtic ones, they were the ones recorded and illustrated in medieval manuscripts.

THE MABINOGION

The most famous of the Celtic legends from Wales were probably written down in the 11th century, but the stories themselves are much older. There are 11 stories altogether, 4 of which relate to Pryderi, an early Prince of Dyfed (in Wales). Arthur also appears in these stories, which were given the name *The Mabinogion* in the 19th century.

THE IRISH LEGENDS

Irish literature gives us the largest number of Celtic legends. Many of them were written down by Christian monks, but even so they tell tales of the old Celtic gods and goddesses, as well as of mortal heroes and heroines. They are one of our best sources for finding out how the Celts looked at life, but, like the stories of King Arthur, they are not a true account of Celtic history.

Many of the Irish legends are contained in several sets of stories, or cycles. One cycle, the "Mythological" cycle, tells of battles between supernatural races who invade Ireland. Another, called the "Ulster" cycle, describes a hero with magical powers, named Cú Chulainn. The "Fenian" or "Ossianic" cycle tells of another hero, named Finn MacCool, his son Oisin (Ossian), and their band of warriors known as the Fianna, or Fenians.

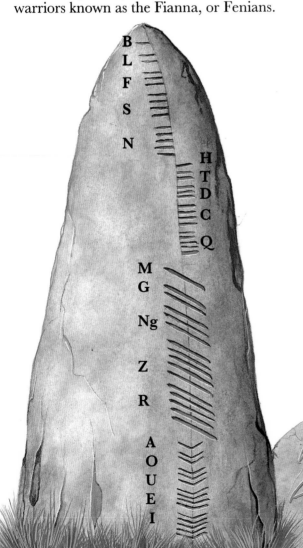

WRITING ON STONES

The Celts also had earlier systems of writing that they used to make memorials for the dead and other inscriptions on stones. The letters were made up of straight lines to make them easy to carve into the stone. The letters used on stones in mainland Europe are largely based on the alphabets used by the people the Celts had the most contact with. Some of the Celts in Britain developed their own alphabets. One alphabet used in Wales was made up of 30 letters, while the Ogham alphabet used in Ireland and western Britain had 25 letters.

This picture of the Irish Celtic hero Ossian was painted in the 19th century. By then his story had changed a lot from the original version. Here he is seen receiving the soul of Napoleon Bonaparte into heaven!

The stone on the left is inscribed with the Ogham alphabet, while the one below shows very early letters that were used by Celts in northern Italy.

CELTIC SURVIVAL

After the conquest of the Celtic lands by the Romans, many Celts adopted Roman ways. The Druids were suppressed and slaughtered, and people were encouraged to practice other religions, including those of the Romans and, later, Christianity. Celtic nobles were allowed to become Roman citizens and officers in the army, and some were even made senators. Many Romans left Italy to live in Hispania (Spain) and Gallia (France), which became two of the richest provinces in the Empire.

ROMANIZATION IN THE WEST

On mainland Europe, "Romanization" was quite thorough. In some of the old Celtic lands, particularly those closest to Rome, Celtic culture disappeared completely. However, in some areas where the Celts had resisted the Roman invasion, the Romans were reluctant to give much power to the local Celts. In these regions the Celts held onto more of their old traditions, and in some places the Celtic way of life remained intact.

SURVIVAL IN BRITAIN

Though most Celts in Britain also adopted Roman ways, many of the Celtic tribes bitterly opposed Roman rule. Therefore, Celtic culture survived more successfully in Britain than on the mainland of Europe. Even in Britain, the survival of the Celtic way of life was strongest in the places that never became part of the Roman Empire or that were only slightly influenced by the Romans. The most important of these were Ireland, which the Romans never visited, and Scotland, which the Romans were never able to conquer. Wales and Cornwall were only on the fringe of Roman influence and also remained strongly Celtic.

In 60 A.D., thousands of Celts, led by Boadicea of the Iceni tribe, revolted against Roman rule in Britain. They attacked and burned the new Roman towns of Colchester, London, and St. Albans, and killed around 70,000 Romans and their supporters, before they themselves were defeated. In Colchester (below), the Roman citizens made a last desperate stand at the Temple of Apollo, a symbol of Roman influence.

The Tara brooch was made in
Ireland in the eighth century A.D.
Its design is still copied today.

THE NEW KINGDOMS

Following the departure of the Romans in
A.D. 410, chaotic times fell on Britain. The
south and east of Britain were invaded by
Angles and Saxons, while the Irish Celts
invaded the west. These Celts were known
as the "Scotti" and they eventually gave
their name to Scotland. Others settled in
Gwynedd and Dyfed (both in Wales), and
from there invaded the regions of Cornwall
and Devon in southwest England. In turn,
Celts from Cornwall and Devon moved to
Gaul and settled in the region called
Armorica. They took their language and
customs with them and the area eventually
developed into an independent state,
which became known as Brittany.

THE CELTIC LANGUAGES

Although the Celtic languages died out in
most of Europe, they survived in Britain,
Ireland, and Brittany. Many of them have
recently undergone a revival as people in
Celtic areas have become more aware of
the importance of their Celtic heritage.
Erse, Gaelic, Cymric (Welsh), and Breton
are still spoken in Ireland, Scotland,
Wales, and Brittany, while Manx, which
was spoken on the Isle of Man, and
Cornish have only recently died out.

*The Celts in Ireland were not directly affected by Roman
rule, but in the ninth century A.D. they suffered raids from the
Vikings. The Vikings later settled on the coast and set up
trading centers at places such as Dublin and Cork. The
Vikings often formed alliances with Irish chieftains, who
were frequently at war with each other.*

PLACE NAMES

Even where
Celtic language
and culture no
longer exist,
the names of
some towns,

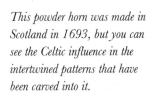

cities, regions, and even countries remind
us of the Celts who once lived there. Paris,
for example, is named after the Parisii
tribe, and Belgium is named after the
Belgii. Lyon in France and London both
take their names from Lugh, the Celtic sun
god. In northwest England, the name
Cumbria is based on the word *Cymry*,
meaning "fellow countrymen."

Although the Romans overwhelmed
the Celts, Celtic influence survives
today—not just in place names and art,
but in the many people who are
descended from the original Celts.

*This powder horn was made in
Scotland in 1693, but you can
see the Celtic influence in the
intertwined patterns that have
been carved into it.*

KEY DATES AND GLOSSARY

Because both the Greeks and the Romans wrote about their encounters with the Celts, we can be sure of the dates of many events from about 300 B.C. onward. Before this time, we have to rely on the work of archaeologists. By doing scientific tests on the artifacts they find, they can tell us when the objects were made, and this in turn tells us when a site was occupied.

At the hilltop oppidum of Alesia the Gallic Celts, led by their chieftain Vercingetorix, made a last great stand against the Romans. Here the Celts are being attacked from behind as they make a desperate attempt to break through the siegeworks built by Julius Caesar's army.

B.C.

750   By this date Celts are living in the Hallstatt area of Austria and becoming wealthy by trading salt.

500   La Tène civilization begins to develop.

c.390 The Celts defeat the Roman army and attack Rome.

298   Celts attack the Oracle at Delphi but are defeated by the Greeks.

278   Around 20,000 Celts fight for Nicomedes of Bithynia against the Syrians. The land they settle in becomes known as Galatia.

225   The Celts suffer a crushing defeat by the Romans at the Battle of Telamon.

224   The Romans invade Cisalpine Gaul.

218   Helped by the Celts, Hannibal's Carthaginian army crosses the Alps to attack the Romans. This begins the Second Punic War.

202   The Romans defeat the Carthaginians at the Battle of Zama, ending the Second Punic War.

198   The Romans set out to conquer Gaul.

197   The Romans take control of Spain.

190   The Galatians ally themselves with the Greeks and are defeated by the Romans at the Battle of Magnesia. Later they ally with the Romans.

121   The Romans take control of Transalpine Gaul.

60   The Boii tribe of Bohemia is defeated by the Dacians.

58   The Helvetii leave their homelands and head towards Gaul. Caesar uses this as an excuse to move his army into Gaul.

55   Most of Gaul is under Roman control. Caesar sends an expedition to Britain but is unable to establish Roman rule there.

52   Celtic resistance in Gaul is crushed at the Battle of Alesia. Vercingetorix surrenders, and is beheaded in 46 B.C.

A.D.

43 Roman conquest of Britain begins.
61 Boadicea leads the Iceni tribe in revolt against Roman rule.
74 Galatia becomes part of the Roman province of Cappadocia.
122 Hadrian's Wall marks the northwest limit of Roman expansion.
312 The Roman Emperor Constantine makes Christianity the official religion of the Empire.
410 The last of the Roman legions leave Britain to defend Rome.
450 By this date, Celts from Britain have settled in Brittany.
c.793 The Viking raids start.
1014 Irish King Brian Ború defeats the Vikings and their allies at Clontarf.

Glossary

artifact: any object that has been made by a person.

barter: to obtain goods by exchanging them for other goods of a similar or higher value.

broch: a stone tower built to protect a Celtic settlement.

fodder: food such as hay that is used to feed animals.

Oracle: one of the most important holy places to the ancient Greeks.

sack: to rob a town or a city, usually with much violence and destruction.

scabbard: the cover made to fit over the blade of a knife or a sword.

spindle and whorl: a weighted stick used to spin a single thread by hand.

wattle-and-daub: building material made by interweaving thin pieces of wood and filling the gaps with mud or plaster.

Quotations

Ammianus Marcellinus was a Roman who wrote about the Celts in the fourth century A.D., when most of the Celtic lands were under Roman rule. Strabo was a Greek geographer who lived from 64 B.C. to A.D. 21. He lived in both Rome and Alexandria, traveled widely, and wrote 17 books on geography. Most of his information on the Celts came from the work of an earlier writer called Posidonius. Diodorus Siculus also wrote in Greek and traced the history of the world up to the end of the Gallic wars in a 40-volume work called *Library of History*. He died in 20 B.C. Lucan was a Roman poet who was born in Spain in A.D. 39. His full name was Marcus Annaeus Lucanus and he died in A.D. 65. Pliny was a Roman scholar and soldier who died in A.D. 79. His 37-volume work, *Natural History*, gave details of the Druids and of Celtic medicine. Julius Caesar, who died in 44 B.C., wrote about the Celts in his work on the Gallic Wars.

INDEX